ALFRED's SACRED PERFORMER COLLECTIONS

MW00699771

ANO

Jazzy Hymns and Spirituals

11 Arrangements of Traditional Favorites

Arranged by Paul Johnston

When asked to play at my church, I often enjoy experimenting with familiar hymns and spirituals. The arrangements in this collection began as an effort to contribute meaningful new music to our church services. With these selections, I have tried to keep the spirit of the original music while incorporating jazz harmonies and written-out "improvised" passages. I also explore different contemporary styles: a stride piano version of "Jesus Loves Me, This I Know," a gospel-flavored "Oh Happy Day," a jazzy "I've Got Peace Like a River," and a funky "Wade in the Water." These pieces range from the reflective to the celebratory, and I hope you enjoy playing them for your own pleasure and to share with others.

Paul Johnston

Alfred Music
P.O. Box 10003
Van Nuys, CA 91410-0003
alfred.com

ISBN-10: 1-4706-1457-X
ISBN-13: 978-1-4706-1457-7

Cover Photos
Stained glass church window in a reddish tone, square orientation © Shutterstock.com / Philip Meyer

(Approx. Performance Time – 2:30)

I've Got Peace Like a River

Traditional
Arr. Paul Johnston

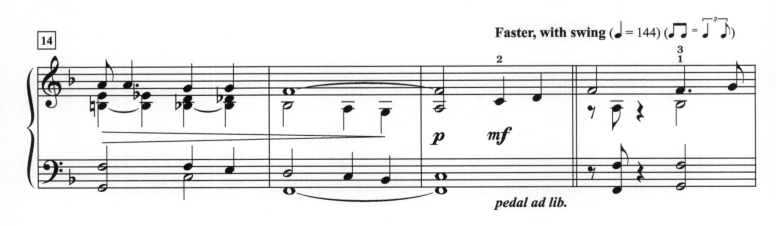

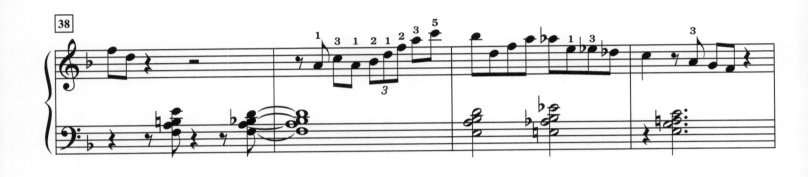

(Approx. Performance Time – 3:00)

Leaning on the Everlasting Arms

Anthony J. Showalter
Arr. Paul Johnston

(Approx. Performance Time — 2:00)

When the Saints Go Marching In

Traditional
Arr. Paul Johnston

(Approx. Performance Time – 2:30)

Jesus Loves Me, This I Know

William B. Bradbury
Arr. Paul Johnston

(Approx. Performance Time – 2:15)

Abide with Me

William Henry Monk
Arr. Paul Johnston

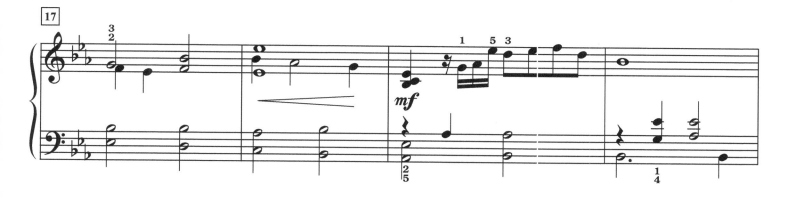

(Approx. Performance Time – 2:30)

Give Me Jesus

Traditional
Arr. Paul Johnston

(Approx. Performance Time – 3:00)

Oh Happy Day

Traditional
Arr. Paul Johnston

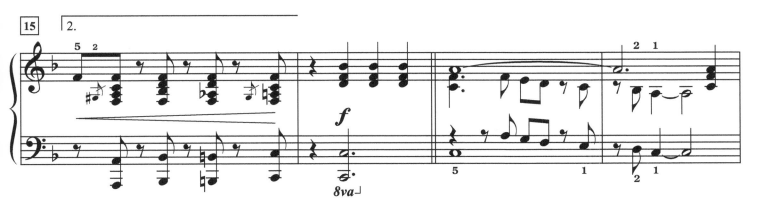

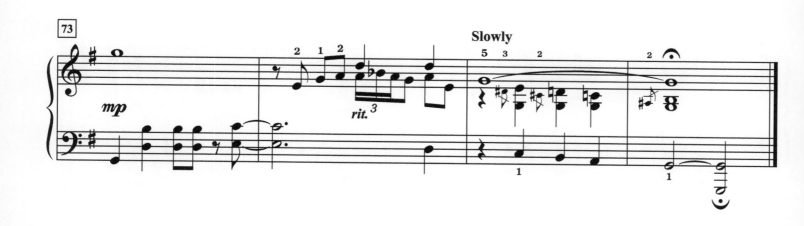

(Approx. Performance Time – 2:45)

Simple Gifts

Joseph Brackett, Jr.
Arr. Paul Johnston

(Approx. Performance Time – 3:15)

Sweet Hour of Prayer

William B. Bradbury
Arr. Paul Johnston

(roll when necessary)

(Approx. Performance Time – 2:15)

Wade in the Water

Spiritual
Arr. Paul Johnston

38

Swing Low, Sweet Chariot

Spiritual
Arr. Paul Johnston

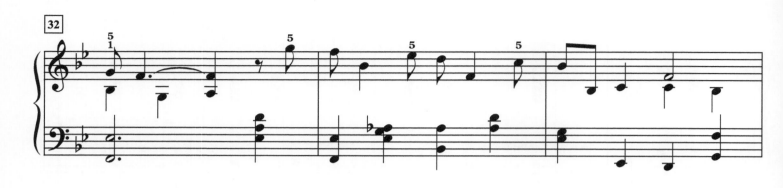